Original title:
The Winter Song

Author: Kätriin Kaldaru
ISBN HARDBACK: 978-9916-79-561-3
ISBN PAPERBACK: 978-9916-79-562-0
ISBN EBOOK: 978-9916-79-563-7

Fragments of a Fickle February

Whispers of winter chill the air,
While sunshine dances, bright and rare.
Snowflakes melt in a sudden blaze,
February, fickle in her ways.

Clouds gather dark, then drift away,
Birds begin to sing and play.
A storm may brew, then clear the sky,
In February's embrace, we sigh.

Days grow longer, shadows shift,
Through warm and cold, we drift adrift.
Hope blooms forth from icy ground,
In the chaos, beauty's found.

The heart flutters like fragile wings,
With every chance that February brings.
Moments flicker, then they fade,
In this short month, love is made.

So here's to February's dance,
In her whimsy, we take a chance.
For in her fickle, tender embrace,
We find the warmth of a fleeting grace.

Chilling Melodies

The wind whispers soft and low,
As snowflakes swirl and dance below.
A haunting tune fills the icy air,
A song of winter, crisp and rare.

Branches bare, they sway and sway,
Inviting chill to come and play.
Notes of frost, a gentle sigh,
In this frozen world, we comply.

A melody sweet, yet bittersweet,
As icy fingers touch our feet.
With every note, a memory stays,
In the heart of winter's haze.

Echoes linger, a shadow's touch,
Reminding us of winter's clutch.
The music fades, yet still we feel,
Chilling melodies that seem so real.

Dance of the Icicles

Icicles hang with shimmering grace,
A frozen ballet in their place.
They twinkle bright, a jeweled show,
As winter's breath begins to blow.

In the dawn, they catch the light,
A crystal dance, pure delight.
Drip by drip, they sway in time,
Nature's rhythm, soft and prime.

The sun peeks out, a warming glance,
Awakening dreams from winter's trance.
The icicles melt, yet leaves a trace,
Of their brief and dazzling grace.

Around them, songs of the cold wind play,
A whispering tune that fades away.
In their falling, a farewell kiss,
The dance of icicles, we shall miss.

Hibernal Lullaby

Snowflakes fall like whispers sweet,
Blanketing earth in soft retreat.
A lullaby of hush and peace,
Where all the restless minds can cease.

The world slows down, a gentle breath,
In winter's arms, a quiet death.
Dreams take flight on frosty nights,
Wrapped in warmth, where hope ignites.

The stars twinkle like dreams held tight,
Guiding souls through the cold night.
A lullaby sung by the moon,
Filling hearts with gentle tunes.

Cradled in blankets, snug and warm,
Away from the chill that brings alarm.
In hibernal embrace we find,
The softness of the winter's mind.

Echoes of a Frosty Dawn

Morning breaks with a silvery hue,
As dawn awakens the day anew.
Frosted fields wear a crystal crown,
Echoes whisper of the night's gown.

Birds take flight, a song unfolds,
In the chilly air, their tales told.
Branches glisten with dewdrops clear,
Awakening life, winter's cheer.

Each breath forms clouds in the air,
A frosty greeting everywhere.
With hearts alive, we step outside,
In echoes where warmth and chill collide.

The beauty found in the quiet light,
Of a frosty dawn, warm and bright.
As shadows retreat and dreams are spun,
We embrace the magic of the sun.

Glacial Tranquility

Silent whispers in the air,
Frozen breath of winter's stare.
Gentle flakes begin to fall,
Nature's peace, a crystal call.

Stillness wraps the world in white,
Stars emerge, a frosty sight.
Moonlight dances on the snow,
In this calm, sweet dreams can grow.

Timeless echoes softly ring,
Winter holds the joy of spring.
In the hush, the heart can rest,
Here, in quiet, we are blessed.

Serenity on the Frosted Path

Footsteps crunch on icy ground,
Whispers soft, no other sound.
Branches glisten, cloaked in white,
Guiding paths through the night.

Every breath a cloud of mist,
Moments like this can't be missed.
Wandering where silence reigns,
Peaceful thoughts in winter's chains.

The stillness touches every soul,
In this world, we feel whole.
Nature's beauty, pure and bright,
Frosted dreams in silver light.

Rhythms of a Cold Heart

Chilled winds bite beneath the skin,
A heart once warm, now locked within.
Echoes of a love long lost,
Winter's grip is worth the cost.

Bitter thoughts like falling leaves,
In the cold, the heart deceives.
Yet, within this frozen space,
A flicker of a warm embrace.

Rhythms of a heartbeat slow,
In the frost, foundations grow.
Ice can melt, and warmth can start,
Resilience blooms within the heart.

A Journey Through the Chill

Icicles hanging from the eaves,
Nature's breath, it gently weaves.
A path unfolds, both dark and bright,
Carving dreams within the night.

Every step, a story told,
In the chill, the heart is bold.
Frosty tales upon the tongue,
Songs of winter, yet unsung.

Mountains rise, their peaks aglow,
Whisper secrets only snow.
Through the chill, my soul will fly,
In the frost, I'm free to cry.

Muffled Footsteps in Snow

Silent echoes in the night,
Footsteps dance, a soft delight.
Blankets white, the world in peace,
Every sound a sweet release.

Moonlight glints on crystal ground,
Whispers linger all around.
Through the trees, a chill breeze flows,
In the dark, the magic grows.

Tracks of life in frosted light,
Stories told in quiet flight.
Shadows stretch with every step,
In winter's hold, our secrets kept.

Stars awaken, keeping guard,
While the night remains on guard.
Each soft crunch a timeless song,
In this moment, we belong.

As the dawn begins to break,
Snowflakes fall, a gentle wake.
Muffled footsteps fade away,
But the memories will stay.

Slate Blue Skies at Dusk

The horizon blushes slow,
Slate blue skies begin to glow.
A canvas vast, the sun's retreat,
Daylight's end, a soft heartbeat.

Whispers of the fading light,
As stars prepare for coming night.
Clouds drift by, a painted stream,
In the dusk, we chase our dream.

Silhouettes of trees align,
Shadows cast like language fine.
Breezes weave through evening's sigh,
Nature speaks, the heart will fly.

Birds call out in fading rays,
Echoes linger, fading days.
Each moment holds a spark divine,
Underneath the vast design.

As twilight wraps the world so tight,
Hope emerges, gentle light.
In slate blue skies, we find our place,
A sacred calm, a soft embrace.

Frosted Whispers

A breath of winter in the air,
Frosted whispers everywhere.
Nature's hush, a frozen spell,
In this silence, dreams do dwell.

Crystal branches sway and dance,
In the stillness, hearts advance.
Every flake a story spun,
Softly falling, one by one.

Underneath a quilted gray,
Time slows down, it melts away.
In this wonder, time stands still,
Peace descends, a sacred thrill.

Footsteps lost, the world awhile,
Wrapped in frost, we find a smile.
Moments freeze, yet love's alive,
In frosted whispers, we survive.

When the dawn begins to rise,
Glimmers peek from chilled blue skies.
Promises of warmth to come,
In frosted whispers, we are home.

Silent Serenade of Snowflakes

Ballet dancers in the air,
Snowflakes twirl without a care.
Glistening in the pale moonlight,
Whispers soft throughout the night.

Each flake falls with gentle grace,
Nature's music, a sweet embrace.
Silently, they drift and sway,
In a world, where dreams can play.

Pillow-soft, the silence grows,
As the earth wears winter's clothes.
Curtains drawn of white delight,
In the hush, our hearts take flight.

A serenade, so soft and light,
Fleeting moments, pure and bright.
Each flake carries tales untold,
In the stillness, warmth unfolds.

When the morning breaks anew,
Snowflakes whisper, skies so blue.
In this moment, time stands still,
Silent serenade, hearts fill.

Celestial Pendants of Ice

Stars twirl in night's embrace,
Frosted whispers trace the space.
Moonlight dances on the ground,
Chilling silence all around.

Glistening gems in the dark,
Nature's art, a frozen spark.
Twilight drapes a silver shawl,
In this wonder, we stand tall.

Crystals hang from branches bare,
A testament, the world so rare.
Time stands still, a breathless pause,
In the beauty, nature's cause.

Veils of mist, like dreams they glide,
Carrying secrets far and wide.
Each icicle, a story told,
In the heart of winter's cold.

Wisp of White

A soft feather in the breeze,
Whispers secrets through the trees.
Dancing lightly, shy and bright,
Bathed in the glow of soft moonlight.

Petals drift, like fleeting sighs,
In the twilight, softly lies.
Gentle as a lover's touch,
Wrapped in silence, oh so much.

Through the haze of morning dew,
Wonders of the world break through.
A single breath, a fleeting glance,
In this moment, hearts entranced.

Clouds descend with softest grace,
Veiling the earth in lace.
Wisp of white, a lullaby,
Calling dreams from night's shy sky.

The Light of Fading Days

Golden hues in twilight kiss,
Shadows stretch with gentle bliss.
Days grow short, as night draws near,
Embers fade, but spirits cheer.

Whispers of what time has brought,
Lessons learned, and battles fought.
In the dusk, a promise stays,
Hope rekindles in fading rays.

A brush of red paints skies anew,
Reflecting dreams that once we knew.
As daylight bids its sweet farewell,
In our hearts, the light will dwell.

Stars ignite in velvet skies,
Embracing all our whispered cries.
In the dark, we find our way,
Guided by the light of day.

Echoes of Enchantment

In the forest, shadows play,
Mysteries weave through the day.
Echoes call from ancient trees,
Carried gently by the breeze.

Moonlit paths that twist and bend,
Where fantasies and real transcend.
Every step a tale unfolds,
Whispers shared, and secrets told.

Glimmers spark in the night air,
Fragrance sweet, a magic rare.
Imagination takes its flight,
In the dance of stars so bright.

Dreamers gather, hearts in sync,
Lost in wonder, breaths they drink.
Through the night, the stories flow,
Weaving threads, where dreams still grow.

Whispering Pines

In the forest deep and wide,
Where the gentle breezes glide,
Whispers echo off the trees,
Carried softly on the breeze.

Sunlight filters through the leaves,
Dancing light that never grieves,
Nature's song a soothing balm,
In the pines, the world is calm.

Birds above begin to call,
Filling spaces, great and small,
Every note a sweet refrain,
In this haven, peace remains.

Mossy carpets underfoot,
Every step a quiet route,
Golden rays through branches shine,
In this realm of peace, divine.

Time fades here, a gentle tide,
In the pines, our hearts abide,
Nature's voice, forever clear,
In the woods, we lose our fear.

Shadows on Ice

Beneath the moon, the lake does gleam,
Reflecting stars that softly beam,
Frozen whispers on the shore,
Echo softly, wanting more.

Footsteps crunch on frosty ground,
Silence wrapped all around,
Shadows dance in silver light,
Embers of a winter night.

Mysteries hidden deep below,
Where the icy currents flow,
Frozen whispers, tales untold,
In this realm, the night grows bold.

Breath hangs heavy in the air,
Every moment, crystalline care,
Magic lingers in this space,
Love and dreams begin to chase.

With each glint of starlit grace,
We find warmth in this cold place,
Shadows on the ice do twine,
In this world, your hand in mine.

Through the Crystal Veil

Gaze beyond the frosted pane,
Where the world wears winter's chain,
Silent whispers in the chill,
Time stands still, a sacred thrill.

Icicles like daggers hang,
Quiet shivers, nature's clang,
Sparkling light, like shards of glass,
In this moment, dreams all pass.

Through the crystal veil we peek,
At the beauty, soft and meek,
Every flake a work of art,
Fleeting moments touch the heart.

Snowflakes dance, a swirling flight,
In the hush of soft twilight,
Whispers carried by the breeze,
Nature's magic, sure to please.

Through the veil, the world transformed,
In the winter, hearts are warmed,
Glistening dreams that gently wail,
In this quiet, through the veil.

Snow-Streaked Solitude

In the landscape, pure and white,
Silence reigns, a soft delight,
Tracks of time in snow condensed,
Whispers of the past, immense.

Frosted trees on every side,
In this beauty, we confide,
Snowflakes fall like gentle sighs,
Kissing earth, as winter nighs.

Echoes lost in endless space,
In this solitude, find grace,
Nature's brush, a calming stroke,
In the snow, the heart awoke.

Beneath the sky, so vast and gray,
Each cold breath leads us away,
To a realm where worries cease,
Here we find our truest peace.

Lost amidst the snow-streaked land,
Holding warmth with every hand,
Solitude, a sweet embrace,
In this magic, find our place.

Chilling Serenade

The wind whispers soft tunes,
Echoes of winter's breath,
Trees sway in the moonlight,
A dance of life and death.

Snow blankets the ground,
Silence reigns supreme,
Footsteps print the white,
Like shadows in a dream.

Fires crackle and pop,
Warmth against the chill,
Stories shared by the hearth,
Time seems to stand still.

Starry skies overhead,
Glistening with delight,
Each twinkle a promise,
Of sweet dreams tonight.

Hearts wrapped in solace,
Laughter fills the air,
Together we find peace,
In this tranquil lair.

Starry Nights of December

The sky shimmers above,
A tapestry of light,
Stars dance in the dark,
A breathtaking sight.

Cold air bites the skin,
But warmth is in our hearts,
Dreams begin to soar,
As the night departs.

Crisp winds weave through trees,
Whispers in the night,
Nature holds its breath,
Awaiting dawn's light.

Each star tells a tale,
Of wishes made in time,
Echoing throughout,
In rhythm and rhyme.

In December's embrace,
We find our place to shine,
Underneath the heavens,
Where our souls align.

The Silent Chill

Frost coats window panes,
Crystals sparkle bright,
A stillness in the air,
Where day meets night.

Muted sounds surround,
Nature's quiet song,
Each breath a soft cloud,
As we move along.

Bare branches reach high,
Against the azure hue,
Life in slumber's grip,
Waiting for something new.

A chill wraps around,
But hearts are warm and free,
In the hush of winter,
We find harmony.

In this tranquil moment,
All worries drift away,
We cherish the silence,
As night turns to day.

Feathered Flakes

Snowflakes fall like whispers,
Softly from the sky,
Each one unique and fleeting,
As time passes by.

Children laugh and play,
Creating art in white,
Building dreams of wonder,
Under the pale light.

The world dons a blanket,
Of shimmering frost,
Each corner transformed,
No beauty left lost.

Footprints mark the path,
Of journeys yet begun,
In this winter wonder,
Where stories wait to run.

As dusk settles in,
And stars begin to gleam,
We savor the moment,
In this snowy dream.

Through the Glimmering Drift

In twilight's dance, the shadows play,
A whispering breeze leads dreams astray.
Through pearled paths where echoes fade,
Glimmers shimmer, love conveyed.

Footsteps softly chart the night,
In silver pools, a world so bright.
Beneath the moon's soft, watchful gaze,
Hearts entwined in moonlit haze.

Waves of starlight gently swell,
Secrets wrapped in silence dwell.
Each breath a story, soft and clear,
Whispers carried, drawing near.

Fragrant blooms in twilight's fold,
Stories waiting to be told.
Through the glimmer, shadows drift,
Life's sweet moments, love's true gift.

In this vast and endless space,
We find our peace, a warm embrace.
Through the glimmer, hand in hand,
Together we explore this land.

Glacier's Penchant

Frozen giants tower high,
Underneath the endless sky.
With whispers low, they crack and creak,
A breath drawn near, the silence speaks.

Frigid blue, a sculptor's touch,
Nature's art, revered so much.
In the field of winter's bloom,
A stark beauty, quiet room.

Time etches deep in ancient ice,
Moments glisten like a slice.
Every shard, a frozen tear,
Glacier's tale, forever near.

Veils of white on mountains steep,
In their shadows, secrets sleep.
With every fall, a story blends,
Glacier's song, a tale that bends.

In the cold where stillness reigns,
Life awaits in icy chains.
From the peaks to valleys low,
Glacier's penchant for the glow.

Silver, Snow, and Solitude

A silver hush on winter's night,
Snowflakes dance in soft twilight.
Each flake a dream, a fleeting sigh,
In solitude, the heart can fly.

Cascades fall with gentle grace,
Nature's cloak, a white embrace.
In silent woods where shadows keep,
The world embraces, drift to sleep.

Footprints lead through glistening trails,
Where the whispering soft wind wails.
With every step, the cold reveals,
In solitude, the spirit heals.

Crystal wonders wrapped in light,
Frozen glimmers melt the night.
Silver dawn breaks, a new refrain,
In solitude, we feel no pain.

Among the trees, a secret song,
Echoes softly, where we belong.
In snow's embrace, hearts intertwine,
Silver moments, forever shine.

Moment of Bated Breath

As time hangs in a fragile thread,
In the stillness, words unsaid.
A heartbeat pauses, eyes wide care,
In this moment, a silent prayer.

The world fades, a distant hum,
Anticipation, a throbbing drum.
In the hush where dreams take flight,
Every whisper ignites the night.

Breath suspended, souls align,
Fingers brush, a spark divine.
In this stillness, truth unfolds,
A tale of love, forever holds.

Glimmers of fate in shadows cast,
Hold the moment, make it last.
With bated breath, we lean and sway,
In this magic, we drift away.

Every glance, a promise made,
In the twilight, fears cascaded.
With hearts ablaze, we stand apart,
This moment carved within our hearts.

Embrace of the White Horizon

Snowflakes dance in silent dreams,
Whispers ride the frigid streams.
A blanket soft, the world reclines,
Underneath the silver signs.

The sun dips low, a glowing thread,
Painting skies with fiery red.
Mountains stand with ghostly grace,
Guardians of this tranquil space.

Footsteps crunch on icy ground,
Echoes of the stillness found.
Nature's breath, a frosty sigh,
Beneath the vast and endless sky.

The horizon beckons, pure and bright,
A canvas kissed by morning light.
Each glimpse a promise to behold,
In the warmth against the cold.

Together we shall brave the freeze,
In this realm of tranquil peace.
With hearts aligned in quiet bliss,
We'll find our soul within the mist.

Tranquil Tundra

In the hush of endless snow,
Quiet valleys gently flow.
Frozen whispers brush the trees,
Carried softly by the breeze.

A world awash in muted hue,
Under skies so vast and blue.
Echoes of the wild remain,
A symphony of sweet refrain.

Boundless stretches, stark yet clear,
Every color crystal sheer.
The Arctic blooms in frozen time,
A serene, untouched rhyme.

Glacial peaks like titans rise,
Guardians under boundless skies.
A tranquil dance of light and shade,
In this icy serenade.

Footprints weave through crystal lands,
Where the silent beauty stands.
In this tundra, spirits soar,
Finding peace forevermore.

Ashes of the Autumn Flame

Leaves cascade like whispered dreams,
Gilded gold in sunlight beams.
Nature's palette, soft and bright,
Fading gently into night.

Embers glow in crisp, cool air,
Colors dance without a care.
The wind carries tales of old,
Of summer warmth and autumn's hold.

Rustling echoes through the trees,
Melodies of drifting breeze.
Rich aromas linger long,
In the heart of nature's song.

Footprints etched in golden trails,
Whispered stories, timeless tales.
Each moment, fleeting like the flame,
As seasons shift and never tame.

With every breath, the world inhales,
The warmth of life, the autumn gales.
As ashes settle, memories stay,
In the dance of night and day.

Glistening Veils Beneath

In the depths of hidden streams,
Glistening veils weave silver dreams.
Reflections shimmer, dance and play,
In the quiet of the day.

Pebbles glint like scattered stars,
Nature's jewels near and far.
Whispering waters slip and slide,
Carving paths with gentle pride.

Mossy banks in emerald tones,
Where the voice of silence roams.
A tapestry of life unfolds,
Rich with secrets yet untold.

Fragrant flowers hint of grace,
Blooming softly in this place.
As the sunbeams kiss the earth,
Every moment sings of birth.

Beneath the surface, life prepares,
An orchestra beyond compare.
In the glistening veils, we see,
The vibrant pulse of harmony.

A Tapestry of Silence

In the hush of the night,
Whispers weave through the air.
Stars twinkle in delight,
As shadows gently stare.

Moonlight drapes the ground,
Softly painting the trees.
A world lost and found,
In the calm of the breeze.

Memories softly flow,
Like rivers in the dark.
Ebbing to and fro,
Casting dreams as a spark.

Silence knows our fears,
In its tender embrace.
Sowing hidden tears,
While time quickens its pace.

In the tapestry spun,
Every thread tells a tale.
Mending hearts just begun,
In the night, we unveil.

Burdened Boughs

Under the weight of time,
Boughs bend with deep despair.
Each leaf tells a rhyme,
Of struggles laid bare.

Whispering in the wind,
They share their heavy load.
Nature holds what's pinned,
On every winding road.

Roots ache beneath the ground,
Anchored in silent dread.
The world's noise profound,
As the weary are fed.

Seasons come and go,
Yet sorrow remains close.
Casting shadows low,
On fields we adore most.

But in the coming spring,
New life begins to bloom.
Hope begins to sing,
Dispelling all the gloom.

Nightingale in the Snow

In winter's crisp embrace,
A nightingale sings sweet.
Echoes fill the space,
Where silence and snow meet.

Feathers kissed by frost,
Notes dance through the air.
A beauty never lost,
In the chill, pure and rare.

Each song a soft glow,
Amidst the cold, dark night.
A warmth in the flow,
Of the bird's gentle flight.

Beneath the silver moon,
A story unfolds slow.
Love's eternal tune,
In the heart's secret glow.

As thaw melts the snow,
The echoes linger on.
In every soft blow,
Joy emerges at dawn.

Ice-Crowned Dreams

Upon the frozen lake,
Dreams lie in crystal sheets.
Each wish a soft ache,
Beneath winter's cool beats.

Glacial whispers call,
Tales of hopes to ignite.
Through the icy thrall,
Spirits soar in flight.

With each step we take,
We tread on fragile ground.
Shivering with the ache,
Of silence all around.

Yet warmth begins to spark,
In the heart's hidden core.
As shadows greet the dark,
We dare to dream once more.

For even in the freeze,
Life breathes beneath the frost.
In the heart's gentle ease,
All hope is never lost.

Enchanted Silence

In the stillness where shadows play,
Whispers of dreams gently sway.
Stars hold secrets, softly gleam,
Night wraps all in a silken dream.

Moonlight dances on silver streams,
Echoes of laughter, starlit beams.
Time stands still, wrapped in a sigh,
In enchanted silence, we fly.

Gentle breezes through branches weave,
Nature's lullaby, we believe.
A world awash in twilight hues,
Silent wonders, we gently choose.

The hush of night, a velvet cloak,
In every heart, a fleeting stroke.
The universe in tender tune,
Awaits the dawn, yet cradles the moon.

When morning breaks, all truth revives,
In whispered dreams, the spirit thrives.
Yet, in the quiet, we find our grace,
In enchanted silence, we embrace.

Frost-Kissed Reverie

Morning glimmers with icy breath,
Nature whispers stories of death.
Frosty patterns, intricate lace,
In every corner, winter's grace.

Branches shimmer, a crystal glow,
Underneath, the soft earth lies low.
The world awakes in a chilly blush,
In quiet moments, time seems to hush.

Footsteps crunch on the powdered snow,
Echoes of laughter with every blow.
Frosted air wraps around with cheer,
In a reverie, I hold you near.

Whispers of winter linger here,
In frozen stillness, we draw near.
A tranquil place, where worries fade,
In frost-kissed dreams, our love parade.

As twilight descends, the stars ignite,
Embraced by the dark, hearts feel light.
In this season, our hopes reside,
In frost-kissed reverie, side by side.

Winter's Soft Kiss

Snowflakes flutter, a gentle fall,
Covering silence, muffling all.
A palette of white, pure and bright,
Winter's soft kiss embraces the night.

Fires crackle, warmth fills the air,
Inside, a haven beyond compare.
Weasting the chill with stories old,
In cozy shadows, we find our gold.

The world transformed, a wonderland,
Crisp and clear, with beauty so grand.
Glistening trees in a crystalline shroud,
Hold hidden dreams beneath the cloud.

Time slows down, as if to pause,
In every breath, a fleeting cause.
Wrapped in blankets, hearts intertwine,
In winter's soft kiss, love will shine.

As dawn approaches, the sun breaks free,
Painting the sky with joyful decree.
Winter departs, but love remains,
In winter's soft kiss, our spirit gains.

A Blanket of Solitude

Wrapped in layers, the world slows down,
A blanket of solitude, nature's gown.
Thoughts drift like clouds on a still, calm sea,
In the quiet, I find pieces of me.

Snow blankets fields and whispers low,
The tranquil hush muffles the glow.
In solitude's hug, I breathe in deep,
Finding solace in moments I keep.

Footprints trace paths on frosty ground,
Echoes of memories, soft and profound.
Time stretches gently, a soothing sigh,
Under the vast, expansive sky.

Here, in the stillness, fears retreat,
In the heart of winter, peace feels sweet.
With each silent hour, I learn to see,
A blanket of solitude comforts me.

As the world awakens, fresh with light,
I carry the calmness, holding it tight.
In every heartbeat, in every breath,
A blanket of solitude conquers death.

Blue Sky Disguised in White

The sky wears a cloak of fluffy white,
Clouds drifting gently in morning light.
A canvas painted with whispers of grace,
Where dreams take flight in this heavenly space.

Beneath the veil, the sun peeks through,
Revealing a world awash in blue.
Textures of hope in the crisp, cool air,
Nature's artistry, beyond compare.

Fleeting shadows dance upon the ground,
As laughter echoes, a sweet, joyful sound.
In the serene stillness, hearts intertwine,
Under the sky, so pure and divine.

Every breeze carries stories untold,
Of whispers from ages, both timid and bold.
In this paradise, we lose all our cares,
Finding solace in the beauty it shares.

Beneath the surface of cottony dreams,
Life flows like rivers, with shimmering gleams.
In moments like these, our spirits unite,
Beneath the blue sky, disguised in white.

Solstice Night's Reverie

Stars flicker softly in the velvet sky,
As the solstice whispers its sweet lullaby.
Night wraps the world in a silken embrace,
Where time dances slowly in cosmic grace.

The moonlight spills like shimmering gold,
Warming the hearts of the young and the old.
Memories linger in the cool midnight air,
Each moment a treasure, precious and rare.

Around the fire, shadows begin to play,
As stories are shared, in a magical sway.
The crackling flames sing a melody bright,
Guiding us through this enchanting night.

In the depths of winter, warmth comes alive,
As we gather together, our spirits revive.
With every heartbeat, the world feels right,
In this solstice night, a shared delight.

Tomorrow brings dawn with its vibrant hues,
But tonight, we revel in the twilight's muse.
For in this moment, we truly belong,
Singing together, our hearts like a song.

Moonlit Blanket

A moonlit blanket wraps the earth tight,
Spreading silver shimmer throughout the night.
Crickets serenade the calm, cool breeze,
While nature sleeps beneath swaying trees.

Stars twinkle gently, each a wish in disguise,
Painting the heavens with hopes that arise.
The world holds its breath in a tranquil trance,
As shadows and dreams begin their dance.

Soft whispers of night drift sweetly near,
With secrets and stories that linger here.
The warmth of the night wraps us in peace,
As worries and burdens softly release.

Under the gaze of a watchful moon,
Hearts intertwine, like a soothing tune.
Lost in the fabric of night's gentle call,
We find our place, knowing love conquers all.

With each fleeting moment, time stands still,
As the moon's tender glow brings us a thrill.
Together we dream, beneath starry skies,
In the moonlit blanket, where magic lies.

Frosty Footprints

In the still of winter, the world feels new,
A frosty canvas glistening with dew.
Every footprint whispers a tale of its own,
Tracing the secrets of paths overgrown.

The air is crisp, tasting of fresh delight,
As children play under the pale moonlight.
Snowflakes twirl softly in a delicate dance,
Painting the earth in a white, dreamy trance.

Each step tells stories of laughter and cheer,
As memories bloom, both far and near.
In the gentle hush that wraps every street,
Frosty footprints fade, yet linger sweet.

Winter's embrace wraps the world so tight,
Creating a wonderland, magical and bright.
With every dawn, the sun's gentle rise,
Erodes the cold, revealing blue skies.

So let us wander 'neath the trees, so grand,
With frosty footprints marking our stand.
In the heart of the season, we find our way,
Celebrating life in a playful display.

Shadows Beneath the Snow

Silent whispers in the night,
Footsteps vanish, out of sight.
Softly draped in winter's cloak,
Secrets linger, hearts bespoke.

Frosted trees, like giants stand,
Guarding dreams from icy hand.
Snowflakes dance, in twinkling light,
Nature's magic, pure delight.

Lost in echoes of the past,
Time drifts slowly, shadows cast.
Beneath the snow, stories sleep,
In frozen silence, memories keep.

As the moonlight softly glows,
Finding warmth where the cold blows.
With every step, the world is new,
Shadows whisper of truths so few.

Nightfall's Glimmer

Stars awaken, one by one,
Nighttime's beauty has begun.
Softly shimmer, gentle glow,
Whispers woven in the flow.

Moonlit paths, a silver thread,
Guiding dreams where angels tread.
Chill in air, a tender kiss,
In this moment, find your bliss.

Dancing shadows, flickering light,
Embrace the calm of starry night.
In the stillness, hearts can soar,
Underneath the skies we explore.

Glimmering secrets, softly shared,
In the silence, we've prepared.
For every wish that takes its flight,
Chase the magic of the night.

Celestial Winter Light

Crystalline frost, a diamond show,
Blankets of white, soft winds blow.
Celestial grace, a tranquil glow,
Winter's wonder in every flow.

Stars nestled in the velvet sky,
Glistening realms where silence lies.
Each breath visible, a fleeting dream,
Nature's canvas, a glimmering theme.

Whispers of snowflakes, soft and bright,
Dance like fairies in the night.
Under the spell of tranquil skies,
Hold your breath as magic flies.

Celestial light, a gentle guide,
Among the trees where shadows hide.
In this stillness, peace ignites,
Illuminating winter nights.

Enchanted Snowfall

Falling feathers, pure and bright,
Whirling softly, dreams take flight.
Nature's art in quiet grace,
Snowflakes twirl in sweet embrace.

Whispers weave through chilled air,
Enchanting moments, beyond compare.
Each flake tells a tale untold,
Of winter nights, and hearts of gold.

Footsteps traced through glittering white,
Chasing shadows in fading light.
Underneath the twilight spell,
Find the magic where dreams dwell.

Glistening paths lead to delight,
In the stillness, spirits ignite.
Embrace the wonder, let it flow,
In the heart of enchanted snow.

Frosted Melodies

In the silence, whispers sway,
Like the snowflakes' gentle play,
Each note a drifting breath,
A dance of life, a song of death.

Beneath the starry, icy veil,
Where nightingale's soft echoes trail,
The moon hums low, a lullaby,
As winter's arms embrace the sky.

Frosted trees in shimmering light,
A symphony of purest white,
Melodies of winter's grace,
In every corner, time slows its pace.

Eager hearts, a tale to weave,
Of blossomed dreams that still believe,
In frosted echoes, peace we find,
In winter's embrace, two souls entwined.

Whispers of the Cold

Gentle breezes tell a tale,
Through icy branches, soft and pale,
Whispers glide on frosted air,
Secrets held with tender care.

The world wrapped in a silver shell,
Every sound a muted bell,
Footsteps hush on crystal ground,
In winter's heart, magic is found.

Shadowed corners, echoes merge,
Nature calls with a quiet urge,
Listen close, for every sigh,
Hides the dreams that never die.

Stars peek through the midnight blue,
While silent thoughts drift like dew,
In this chill, our spirits soar,
As whispers of the cold explore.

Silhouettes in Snow

Silent figures slowly roam,
Across the whitened fields, their home,
Shapes of life in frozen frames,
Caught in winter's stillness, names.

Soft and quiet, shadows blend,
Where icy paths twist and bend,
Every step a story told,
In landscapes of the deep, subdued cold.

Gentle hues of grey and white,
Silhouettes in fading light,
Trace the beauty of the night,
As frosty air ignites delight.

Here we wander, hearts aglow,
In the whispers of falling snow,
Moments captured, time stands still,
In the silence, dreams fulfill.

Dance of the Frost

Frosted fingers touch the dawn,
As daylight slowly wends along,
Dancing lightly, cold and bright,
With every step, the world ignites.

Icicles shimmer, twinkling fair,
In the chill, they paint the air,
Nature's ballet, delicate thrill,
Every movement, a quiet chill.

Underneath the azure dome,
Frost finds beauty, chills the bone,
A waltz of winter, fresh and bold,
In shimmering grace, stories unfold.

Gather 'round, let spirits sway,
In the dance of frosty play,
Together, hearts join in the fun,
As snowflakes glitter in the sun.

Radiance in the Gloom

In shadows deep, a glow appears,
A whispered light that chases fears.
Through tangled roots, it finds a way,
To turn the night to brighter day.

Beneath the stars, the heart takes flight,
Embracing warmth, defying night.
With every spark, a promise grows,
In silence soft, the radiance glows.

Like fireflies dancing in the dark,
They sing a tune, ignite a spark.
A beacon for the lost to find,
In Gloom's embrace, the light aligned.

Each flicker tells a story bold,
Of dreams unveiled, of truths retold.
As shadows fade and spirits bloom,
We walk with grace, dispelling gloom.

With every dawn, a new debut,
Radiance claims the morning dew.
So let your heart, unbound, ascend,
In every loss, find light to mend.

Frost's Gentle Touch

In the early dawn, a coat of white,
Every blade glimmers, pure delight.
Nature dons her frosted veil,
A tranquil world, serene and pale.

Whispers of ice upon the air,
Crystal lace woven with care.
Trees adorned like jeweled crowns,
Silent beauty in snowy towns.

Footsteps muffled, a gentle sound,
Each step a softness on the ground.
The world transformed in winter's grace,
Frost's gentle touch, a soft embrace.

Throughout the day, the sun will gleam,
Chasing shadows, warming dreams.
Yet as night falls, the frost will cling,
A quiet peace in everything.

In nature's breath, a soothing hush,
Time holds still in winter's rush.
With every flake, a new design,
Frost's gentle touch, so divine.

Moonlit Reflections

Upon the lake, the moonlight spills,
A silver path on quiet hills.
The waters dance with dreams untold,
In night's embrace, the heart grows bold.

Whispers of night breeze through the trees,
Carrying secrets on the breeze.
A mirror held to sky's deep face,
Each ripple shows a world's grace.

Stars twinkle like the eyes of dreams,
Painting starlight in gentle beams.
The silver glow, a soft caress,
In moonlit realms, we find our rest.

With every wave, a story flows,
In tranquil nights, true beauty grows.
Reflections mirror hopes anew,
In every glimpse, our spirits flew.

As dawn approaches, shadows fade,
But memories of night won't trade.
For in the calm of silvery nights,
We found our place in endless sights.

Nature's Frosted Choir

In winter's grasp, the silence hums,
A frosty breath, the stillness comes.
Each flake a note of beauty rare,
In nature's choir, a song to share.

The trees hold hands with icy grace,
Embracing cold in their embrace.
Whispers float on crisp, clear air,
As winter winds weave tunes to spare.

From snowy peaks to valleys low,
Each sound a testament to snow.
A gentle rustle, a soft sigh,
Nature sings beneath the sky.

In every gust, a harmony,
Of life and stillness, wild and free.
The world adorned in fleeting white,
Nature's choir, a pure delight.

As seasons shift, the choir will change,
Yet in the frost, we find the strange.
For every note, both soft and clear,
Nature's song is always near.

Echoes in the Evergreen

In the forest deep and wide,
Where shadows dance and trees abide,
The whispers of the leaves resound,
A haunting song from ground to ground.

Sunlight filters through the green,
Painting scenes that dance and glean,
Each breeze carries tales of yore,
Of weary travelers and lore.

Branches sway in harmony,
Nature's soft cacophony,
Echoes linger in the air,
Filling hearts with gentle care.

A carpet bright of moss and fern,
In every nook, the heart can yearn,
To find a peace, a place of rest,
In evergreen, the soul is blessed.

Among the trunks, a secret lies,
Where dreams awaken, never die,
Beneath the boughs, the world feels right,
In this embrace of soft twilight.

Whispers Beneath the Snow-Draped Sky

Silent flakes begin to fall,
A curtain soft that blankets all,
Whispers hidden, secrets deep,
While the world is lulled to sleep.

The quiet hum of chilly air,
Carrying wishes everywhere,
Each flurry dances, light and free,
In winter's grasp, we find the key.

Footprints trace a path anew,
Across the white, where all is true,
Voices quiet, moments shared,
In this bliss, we are prepared.

Stars emerge in twilight's guise,
Glistening like hope in the skies,
Beneath the snow, life sighs and breathes,
In the stillness, magic weaves.

Dreams unfold in softest light,
As shadows dance with pure delight,
Beneath the snow, a world of charms,
Embraces us in soothing arms.

Flurries of Lost Time

Days drift like leaves on a stream,
Carried away in a wistful dream,
Moments fleeting, like whispers near,
Echoes of laughter that disappear.

A dance of hours, swift and bright,
Gliding softly from day to night,
Each second a snowflake, unique and rare,
Fleeting yet precious, suspended in air.

Time weaves a tale that cannot hold,
Stories hidden, memories bold,
Flurries swirl in the winter's chill,
A tapestry woven with dreams to fulfill.

In the stillness, we grasp at threads,
Of moments lost, where the heart treads,
Each memory glimmers, a treasure untold,
In flurries of time, our dreams unfold.

We chase the shadows, we long to find,
The threads of our life, intertwined,
In the flurries that swirl and sway,
We gather the pieces, come what may.

Frosty Filigree

On windows clear, a pattern grows,
Delicate lace that nature sews,
Frosty filigree, a transient art,
Whispers of winter, soothing the heart.

Each crystal twinkles, a story spun,
Of chilly nights and warming sun,
A tapestry crafted, fine and bright,
Dancing softly in morning light.

As the dawn awakens the world anew,
Frost gives way to a gentle hue,
But in its wake, a memory stays,
Of nature's touch in fleeting ways.

With every breath, we trace the line,
Of icy whispers, so divine,
A moment captured, a tale conveyed,
In frosty filigree's soft parade.

So let us cherish this transient gift,
In every pattern, our spirits lift,
For as the warmth of spring draws near,
We'll hold these whispers, soft and clear.

Arctic Whispers

Beneath the pale, shimmering sky,
Silent secrets drift and sigh.
The cold winds sing a gentle tune,
In the heart of winter, by the moon.

Snowflakes dance in twilight's glow,
Footprints blanketed by white below.
Stars above twinkle, bright and clear,
In the arctic's embrace, all is near.

Icy breath of the ancient night,
Nature's echo, pure delight.
Whispers carried on the breeze,
Softly stirring the frozen trees.

Glaciers whisper tales of old,
In frozen realms, the stories unfold.
Echoing through the vast expanse,
Life beneath the ice does dance.

Awake beneath the shimmering frost,
Beauty found, never lost.
In the stillness, peace takes flight,
A world of wonder, pure and bright.

Frosted Footsteps

In the quiet of the early morn,
Frosted paths, the world reborn.
Every step on glistening ground,
Whispers of warmth, lost, yet found.

Crystals shimmer on branches bare,
Nature's art, a crafted rare.
Breath visible in the sleepy air,
Footsteps echo, a soft prayer.

Winds caress with icy breath,
In this stillness, there's no death.
Life holds on in subtle ways,
Through frosted nights and winter days.

Silence blankets the earth so white,
Fires crackling, hearts feel light.
In the chill, a warmth resides,
In every corner, magic hides.

With each turn upon this ground,
Nature's beauty can be found.
Frosted footsteps lead us through,
Into a world both fresh and new.

Shards of Ice and Light

Shards of ice catch the sun's embrace,
Glistening jewels in a frozen space.
Colors dance in the morning dew,
A mosaic crafted, bright and true.

Nature's canvas, carved from time,
Each fragment sings a silent rhyme.
Frozen whispers in the air,
Echoing moments beyond compare.

Radiance falls on a blanket white,
Transforming day into the night.
Every sparkle tells a tale,
Of winter's grace, where dreams prevail.

In this realm of ice and sheen,
Beauty so pure, almost unseen.
Fragile moments, so divine,
In the shards of ice, light aligns.

As the sun begins to wane,
Shimmering hues drive soaked refrain.
In the depths of winter's heart,
A masterpiece, nature's art.

Whispering Pines

In the forest where the pines sway,
Whispers weave through the light of day.
Branches dance with a gentle grace,
Nature's quiet, sacred space.

Among the needles, secrets lie,
Tales of earth, the wind, the sky.
Rustling leaves sing songs so pure,
In these woods, the soul finds cure.

Beneath the boughs, shadows play,
In the stillness, hearts will say,
Every breath, a note in tune,
Echoing softly beneath the moon.

Pine scents curl in the misty air,
Filling lungs with a tranquil flare.
Promises made in the soft light,
In whispering pines, all feels right.

So wander deep where the tall trees stand,
Feel the whispers, hand in hand.
For in their heart, wisdom lies,
In the pines' embrace, the spirit flies.

Cascading Crystals

In twilight's soft embrace, they gleam,
Nature's jewels, a sparkling dream.
Flowing down with graceful ease,
Whispering winds through the trees.

Each drop a story, each fall a song,
A dance of light where they belong.
They shimmer bright 'neath the moon's gaze,
Unfolding magic in a haze.

A crystal stream that never sleeps,
Awakening secrets that the forest keeps.
With every sparkle, hearts take flight,
In a world woven pure and white.

Catch the glow as the sun breaks free,
Painting the frost on each leaf and tree.
A moment held, a treasure found,
In cascading crystals, joy unbound.

Let us wander through this enchanting night,
Where whispers of beauty shine so bright.
In nature's arms, let us be still,
As cascading crystals weave their thrill.

A Symphony of Silence

In the stillness, whispers play,
A symphony in soft array.
Echoes linger in the air,
A melody beyond compare.

Each note a breath, a moment caught,
In quietude, we seek what's sought.
Time slows down, the world retreats,
In silence, harmony completes.

The rustling leaves, a gentle sigh,
Nature's song, a lullaby.
Stars twinkle in a velvet black,
Guiding dreams upon their track.

Close your eyes and feel the beat,
Listen closely, hear it sweet.
In the void where thoughts dissolve,
A symphony we all involve.

A harmony that knows no end,
In silence, our hearts blend.
Music flows in hidden streams,
Crafting life from unvoiced dreams.

Delicate Frost on the Window

A crystal lace adorns the glass,
Delicate whispers as moments pass.
Nature's brush paints a fleeting scene,
A winter's charm, serene, pristine.

Glistening patterns, intricate and bright,
Drawing the dawn with a soft light.
Inside, we warm by the flickering flame,
While frosted art plays its silent game.

Each flake a memory, unique and true,
Merging with dreams, both old and new.
The world outside wears a shimm'ring coat,
While stillness wades in a silent boat.

As daylight creeps through the morning haze,
The frost begins to shyly phase.
But every drop tells a tale of cold,
A frosted bond that never grows old.

In these moments, we find our peace,
As winter's magic offers release.
With delicate frost, the window gleams,
Whispering secrets, holding dreams.

The Breaths Between Seasons

In the hush where moments pause,
Nature ponders, without a cause.
The breath between the falling leaves,
Where time holds tightly what it grieves.

Spring's fresh whispers, soft and new,
Meet autumn's sighs with a gentle view.
A tapestry woven in shades of gold,
The stories of life in silence told.

With every heartbeat, cycles shift,
In the dance of time, we find our gift.
Memories linger, like shadows cast,
In the folds of the present, future, past.

When winter fades and summer gleams,
In those spaces lie our dreams.
The breaths between lay treasures bare,
In fleeting moments, love is shared.

So let us cherish, in ebb and flow,
The gentle breaths, the seeds we sow.
For in each season, we find our place,
In nature's heart, in time's embrace.

Echoes of a Frozen Sky

Whispers dance on frosty air,
Stars blink softly, unaware.
Moonlight spills on glistening ground,
In silence, the cosmos is found.

Frosted trees stand tall and proud,
Wrapped in nature's chilling shroud.
Each snowflake a story untold,
A masterpiece of shimmering gold.

Silent nights, with echoes clear,
Every heartbeat draws us near.
In the stillness, feelings bloom,
Winter's magic, a silent loom.

An endless sky of dreams to share,
Haloed light, a silver flare.
In freezing breath, we find our tune,
Echoes softly 'neath the moon.

Time suspends in frozen grace,
In each moment, we embrace.
The night is young, the starry high,
We are children of the sky.

Hibernal Lullabies

Snowflakes fall like whispered dreams,
Wrapped in warmth, the soft light gleams.
Under blankets, hearts entwine,
In hibernation, souls align.

The world outside is painted white,
A canvas of the quiet night.
While nature sleeps, we gently sigh,
To the tune of the winter sky.

Crackling fires and shadows dance,
Nature's lullaby, a soothing trance.
Each note a memory in the air,
Curling softly, without a care.

Sleepy whispers fill the room,
Carried softly, like a bloom.
In dreams of snow, we drift away,
Till dawn brings back the day.

Time may freeze, but love runs deep,
In winter's arms, we softly sleep.
Hibernal hush, the world so still,
A cherished peace, a quiet thrill.

Crystal Harmonies

Every note, a dance of light,
Whispers of the frosty night.
Icicles hang like crystal bells,
Telling tales the silence swells.

Beneath the surface, magic plays,
In the shimmer, time delays.
Winter's breath, a gentle song,
In this realm, we all belong.

Snowflakes swirl in graceful lines,
Nature weaving secret signs.
Each crystal harmony resounds,
In hidden echoes, love abounds.

The moon weaves through the frosty air,
A melody beyond compare.
Through the night, the magic flows,
In the cold, our spirit glows.

Every heartbeat finds its place,
In the heart of winter's grace.
Here we dance, like falling snow,
In this crystal dream we know.

Beneath the Icy Veil

An unseen world beneath the ice,
Where whispers mingle, cold and nice.
The earth sleeps deep in winter's hold,
A tale of warmth yet to be told.

Frozen streams and crystals bright,
Dance beneath the silver light.
Life awaits, in tranquil dreams,
Beneath the surface, hope still gleams.

In silence vast, the secrets lie,
Waiting for the sun to pry.
With every thaw, a new reveal,
Life awakens, beneath the veil.

The gentle touch of springtime's breath,
Will awaken, the dance of death.
Yet for now, we embrace the freeze,
In winter's hush, we find our peace.

Each layer holds a promise dear,
A softer world will soon appear.
Beneath the icy veil we wait,
For life to bloom, it's never late.

Tapestry of Frost and Flame

In the dawn, where shadows play,
Whispers dance in hues of gray.
Frost and flame intertwine bright,
Creating warmth in the chill of night.

Embers glow beneath the frost,
Hope revived, no moment lost.
Nature weaves her bold design,
With threads of fire, pure and fine.

Across the fields, the colors clash,
Crisp and warm in a spirited dash.
The tapestry unfolds with grace,
A world of wonder, a sacred space.

Beneath the heavens, wild and free,
Life ignites in lush decree.
Frosty mornings birthed anew,
Scattered dreams in blazing hue.

As twilight falls, the canvas glows,
Embers flicker, beauty flows.
In every corner, warmth remains,
A tapestry of frost and flames.

The Chill of Yearning

Deep in the woods, silence sighs,
Underneath the starlit skies.
A whisper calls, each breath a plea,
The chill of yearning, wild and free.

Branches bare with dreams untold,
Memories wrapped in shards of cold.
Hearts beat slow, as shadows dance,
In the stillness, I take a chance.

Winter's breath upon my face,
A reminder of love's embrace.
Through frosted air, a longing stirs,
Echoes of warmth in gentle murmurs.

As frost bites down and stars ignite,
I search for love beneath the night.
Every sigh, a plea to the air,
In the chill, I find you there.

Time moves slow, yet spirits rise,
In the silence, I hear your lies.
Beneath the stars, the longing grows,
A bitter sweet where yearning flows.

Beneath the Silent Stars

Beneath the silent stars so bright,
Whispers of dreams dance in the night.
Each twinkle holds a tale untold,
Stories alive, both warm and cold.

The moonlit path, a guide so clear,
Invites the heart to release its fear.
With every step, a secret shared,
The universe wraps those who dared.

In the quiet, echoes take flight,
Memories linger, shadows ignite.
Time stands still in the night's embrace,
A timeless bond in this sacred space.

Stars align as wishes unfold,
A tapestry of hearts, pure gold.
Together we weave in this vast expanse,
Beneath the quiet, the stars' soft dance.

In the darkness, we find our way,
Twilight whispers, night turns to day.
Beneath the silent stars, we roam,
Finding a forever, a place called home.

Enigma of the Frosted Night

In the enigma of the frosted night,
Where shadows creep beyond the light.
A world adorned in icy lace,
Mysteries linger in every space.

Footsteps echo, crisp and low,
Breath hangs heavy, a gentle glow.
Each step reveals a secret path,
A place where silence feels the wrath.

The stars above, a shimmering veil,
Guarding whispers of the gale.
As frost embraces every tree,
Nature's riddle, wild and free.

Time flows slow in this tranquil scene,
Every moment, a precious dream.
In the quiet, stories spark,
In the darkened woods, we leave our mark.

Beneath the moon, shadows entwine,
The frosted night, a tale divine.
In every breath, a promise found,
An enigma that knows no bound.

Frost-kissed Dreams

In the quiet of the night,
Whispers of frost take flight.
Wrapped in blankets, warm and tight,
Dreams dance under moonlight.

Frozen breath upon the air,
Sparkles glinting everywhere.
A world transformed, so rare,
Glimmers of magic, we share.

Crisp and clear, the shadows play,
Each flake unique in its own way.
Nature's canvas, cold and gray,
Tomorrow's dawn will brighten the day.

Quiet echoes in the still,
Filling hearts with winter's thrill.
Let the frost beneath us spill,
As dreams are born, and time stands still.

So here we lie, together near,
Chasing dreams without fear.
In this moment, crystal clear,
Frost-kissed dreams, we hold dear.

Stillness in the White

Blankets draped on Earth's wide face,
Whispers of winter's soft embrace.
A serene, untouched space,
Stillness wrapped in gentle grace.

Footsteps muffled in the snow,
A hush that follows, soft and slow.
Nature pauses, time won't flow,
In this calm, our hearts will grow.

Lone branches bow, a silent prayer,
Nature's art, delicate and rare.
The world adorned with frosty wear,
In the quiet, beauty's flare.

Crystal stars in the evening glow,
The cold air carries whispers low.
Breath appears like mist in tow,
In this stillness, souls will know.

Moments linger, we invite,
Life is pure in the moonlight.
Together here, hearts feel so right,
In this stillness, pure delight.

Serenading the Stars

On frigid nights with skies so clear,
Soft lullabies that draw us near.
Each twinkling light, a song we hear,
Whispers of dreams we hold so dear.

The galaxy spins, a wondrous sight,
Guiding wanderers with its light.
In the vastness, hearts take flight,
Chasing shadows of the night.

Constellations weave timeless tales,
Across the dark, the starlight sails.
In their glow, the spirit prevails,
Mapping dreams where love prevails.

Dance of cosmic serenade,
Where hopes and wishes don't evade.
In the sky, our fears are laid,
Under the stars, our bond is made.

So here we stand, in awe we gaze,
Heartbeats echo in endless ways.
In this moment, life's gentle haze,
Serenading stars, through night we blaze.

Winter's Embrace

Snowflakes fall like softest sighs,
Whispers woven in chilly skies.
In winter's arms, the world complies,
Finding warmth as time softly flies.

Branches bow with a heavy load,
Nature's quilt, a silence rode.
In this beauty, hearts feel flowed,
In winter's grasp, we wrote our code.

Cozy fires knit stories told,
Of frosty nights and spirits bold.
In icy realms, our dreams unfold,
Creating warmth, a love retold.

Each breath a cloud in the frigid air,
We find connection, hearts laid bare.
In this stillness, we become aware,
Of winter's love that we all share.

Beneath the stars, so vast and wide,
In winter's embrace, we take pride.
Together in this quiet ride,
In nature's arms, we will abide.

Snowbound Harmonies

In the hush of winter's grace,
Softly falls the pure white lace.
Whispers dance upon the breeze,
Nature's song, a symphony of trees.

Footprints trace the crystal path,
Echoes of the hearth's warm bath.
Frosty breath in the biting air,
Silent secrets linger there.

Candles flicker, shadows play,
As twilight forms a soft ballet.
The stars emerge in velvet sky,
While snowflakes twirl and gently sigh.

Gathered near, hearts intertwine,
Sipping cocoa, feeling fine.
Laughter weaves through frosty nights,
Sharing dreams by candlelights.

In this world, so calm and bright,
Snowbound harmonies take flight.
Wrapped in warmth, our spirits soar,
Together here, forevermore.

A Glimpse of the Hearth

Embers glow in cozy night,
Crackling wood, a heart's delight.
Shadows dance upon the wall,
In the warmth, we find our all.

Through the window, snowflakes fall,
Nature's blanket, soft and small.
Inside, the laughter flows like wine,
A glimpse of joy, where hearts align.

Kettle sings, a calming tune,
Under the watchful, silent moon.
Stories shared in candle's light,
Gathered close, our souls take flight.

Memories linger, richly spun,
Each moment cherished, every one.
As winter wraps its chill around,
We find our peace, our love profound.

A glimpse of the hearth, where dreams ignite,
In every corner, hope shines bright.
Together, we create our song,
In warmth and love, we all belong.

Celestial Drift of Snow

High above, the heavens sigh,
Snowflakes twirl, and softly fly.
Casting whispers in the air,
A celestial drift, beyond compare.

Moonlight bathes the world in white,
Stars awaken, shining bright.
Each flake, a unique design,
Falling gently, so divine.

Trees adorned in twinkling light,
Nature's beauty, pure delight.
As the ground wears a frosty gown,
The earth transforms, a jeweled crown.

In this silence, dreams take form,
Wrapped in peace, we feel the warm.
Celestial wonders in our sight,
Snowflakes swirling through the night.

With every drift, our spirits rise,
Touched by magic, we realize.
In this dance of winter's glow,
We find comfort in the snow.

Solitary Pine's Tune

In the woods, a lone pine stands,
Whispering secrets of distant lands.
Beneath its boughs, the world feels still,
Listening close, we share its will.

Branches sway with gentle grace,
A melody of time and space.
In the silence, wise and deep,
The pine holds dreams we wish to keep.

Snow sits soft upon its arms,
Nature's blanket, full of charms.
Against the cold, it stands alone,
A guardian, proud, and overgrown.

With every wind that bends the tree,
A tune flows softly, wild and free.
Echoes of the past resound,
In the heart of winter's ground.

Solitary pine, you sing your song,
In your embrace, we feel we belong.
Through seasons' change, you remain true,
A steadfast friend, forever you.

Crystal Chimes in the Air

Soft whispers dance with the breeze,
Bells ring sweetly in the trees.
Dewdrops glisten in morning light,
Each note a jewel, pure and bright.

Fluttering wings of a fleeting dove,
Serenades sung, wrapped in love.
Echoes linger, a soothing balm,
In the silence, hearts grow calm.

Sunlight shimmers, the world awakes,
Joyful laughter, the earth it shakes.
Harmonies weave through skies so wide,
In this moment, all joys confide.

Journeys began with crystal tones,
Melodies shared like whispered loans.
Nature's rhythm, a gentle guide,
In this symphony, we all abide.

As daylight fades, night gently falls,
The stars emerge, answering calls.
Chimes now silent, dreams take flight,
In the stillness, all feels right.

Gentle Frost's Embrace

Morning light on a velvet bed,
Sparks of silver, where shadows tread.
Every blade with a soft caress,
Nature's cloak, a moment's dress.

Whispers soft through the trees so bare,
A chill that lingers in the air.
Raindrops freeze on the windowpane,
Comets of ice in the winter's reign.

Crystals form on each chilled branch,
Glimmers cast in a frosty dance.
Quiet moments, the world holds still,
In this wonder, our hearts fulfill.

Clouds gather as twilight descends,
The frost-kissed earth, where magic bends.
Stars above twinkle like the frost,
In nature's arms, we're never lost.

Wrapped in warmth from the winter's breath,
Every heartbeat defies the death.
In gentle frost, we find our grace,
A tender touch, a warm embrace.

Frostbitten Hymn

Cold winds sing through the frozen pines,
Each note a story, a tale entwines.
Voices rise from the snowy ground,
In this silence, pure joy is found.

Footsteps crunch on the glittering snow,
Whispered secrets the shadows bestow.
Every flake tells a fragment of light,
In their descent, they dance with delight.

Icicles hang like crystal tears,
Harvesting dreams through the frozen years.
A symphony played by the winter's breath,
A melody soft, yet hinting at death.

Under the stars, the night grows cold,
Wrapped in time, we gather our bold.
Frostbitten hymns in the stillness rise,
A heart-warming echo beneath the skies.

Beneath the blanket, the world sleeps tight,
In the arms of frost, we find our light.
As dawn breaks, the hymn softly fades,
Yet in our souls, the song cascades.

Yule's Gentle Breath

Candles flicker in the evening glow,
Softly warming the spirits below.
Garlands hang with a festive cheer,
Yule's embrace brings love ever near.

Cinnamon whispers, pine scents the air,
Joy and laughter fill every chair.
Crackling hearth with stories to tell,
In cozy corners, we weave our spell.

Stars above twinkle, bright as dreams,
Moonlight dances on frosty streams.
The night stretches with magical grace,
In every heart, there's a peaceful place.

Gifts exchanged with grateful hands,
Sharing memories that time withstands.
In this season of warmth and light,
Hope springs forth, banishing night.

As Yule's breath sighs through the trees,
Embracing warmth in the winter freeze.
Together we stand, hand in hand,
In love's embrace, our spirits grand.

Echoes Beneath the Starry Sky

Whispers dance on the evening breeze,
While shadows play among the trees.
Stars glimmer like secrets untold,
Each one a dream that dares to unfold.

Underneath the vast, endless dome,
We find in the night a place called home.
The moon casts her light on the sleeping earth,
Reminding us all of our endless worth.

Echoes of laughter, soft and clear,
Bounce off the silence, drawing near.
Nature sings out in a jubilant tune,
Lulling our hearts in the light of the moon.

In moments like these, we feel alive,
As stars overhead gently thrive.
Every glimmer holds a story bright,
Unveiling the magic of a starry night.

So let us wander, hand in hand,
Through the wonders of this starlit land.
For beneath the vastness, we realize,
We are the echoes beneath the skies.

Winding Trails of White

Footprints carved in the soft, fresh snow,
Lead us where the wild winds blow.
Through the forest, silent and deep,
In winter's hush, the world is asleep.

Boughs heavy with jewels of ice,
Glisten and shimmer, a frosty paradise.
Each bend in the path tells a new tale,
Of journeys ventured without fail.

The air crisp bites, as we move with grace,
Every breath reveals this serene place.
In the stillness, our worries fade,
As the beauty of winter thoughtfully invade.

Winding trails of white call us near,
To embrace the quiet that we hold dear.
With every step, the moment we share,
Reminds us of magic, beyond compare.

As dusk descends, shadows grow long,
Wrapped in twilight's soft, soothing song.
In the glow of the moon's gentle light,
We treasure the trails that feel just right.

A Symphony of Chill

Frost-kissed mornings, a hush in the air,
Nature adorned in her cold, white flare.
Whispers of winter echo so clear,
In the symphony of chill, we draw near.

Winds weave through branches with gentle sighs,
As the sun peers through the gray, weary skies.
A twirl of snowflakes, they dance and play,
In the cold embrace of a winter's day.

Crackling fires at the end of the road,
Welcome us back from the chill and the cold.
Hot cocoa steaming, a cozy delight,
Reminding us all of the warmth found at night.

In the silence of frost, we find our peace,
As winter's symphony whispers and may cease.
Yet in the stillness, we dream and we play,
Inspired by the magic that winter displays.

So let the chill wrap us like a song,
In the heart of the season, we all belong.
As the chill of the night brings us together,
We embrace the joy in the cool, crisp weather.

A Hearthside Memory

Flickering flames, a warm tender glow,
Imprints of laughter, soft tales to bestow.
Gathered together, with loved ones in sight,
In the embrace of the hearth, we find our light.

The crackle of wood sets the evening's pace,
Each moment shared, a sweet, cherished space.
Old stories told with nostalgic delight,
Echoes of joy in the flickering light.

Hands wrapped around mugs, smiles all around,
In this cozy haven, solace is found.
Whispers of love in the glow of the fire,
Igniting in hearts a warm, deep desire.

The seasons may change, yet this memory stays,
A balm for the soul through life's winding ways.
For in the heart's warmth, we create and we mend,
A tapestry woven, with family and friends.

So let us return to that friendly embrace,
Where laughter and warmth fill the open space.
A hearthside memory, eternally dear,
Forever a treasure, always near.

An Elegy of Frost

Beneath the pale and distant stars,
The whispers of the cold night breeze,
Each breath a ghost, a memory,
Of warmth lost in frozen seas.

The branches shiver, bare and still,
With crystals clinging to their frame,
Nature's sigh, a silent chill,
Reminds us well of winter's claim.

A blanket white upon the ground,
Soft silence wraps the sleeping earth,
In solitude, where dreams are found,
The frost reveals a fleeting girth.

Yet in this icy, waning light,
A beauty glows in frosted hue,
Though everything is touched by night,
A memory lingers, pure and true.

So let us walk this frozen path,
With hearts entwined though cold may reign,
For in the frost, we'll find our wrath,
Yet also love within this pain.

Shimmering Silence

In twilight's grasp, the world stands still,
A whispered hush drapes over all,
Each leaf and branch, a frozen thrill,
In shimmering silence, softly call.

Stars twinkle bright in the velvet night,
As echoes of the day retreat,
The moon bestows its silvery light,
While shadows dance on quiet street.

The gentle hush of drifting snow,
Wraps the earth in a soft embrace,
A blanket where dreams come to grow,
In winter's love, we find our place.

The heartbeats pulse in tender time,
Within this stillness, peace we seek,
Amidst the calm, our thoughts can climb,
To heights where silence dares to speak.

And as the dawn begins to rise,
The shimmering gives way to day,
But in our hearts, the night defies,
To linger softly, then decay.

Veil of the Pale Sun

Behind the mist, the pale sun glows,
A quiet warmth in morning's dew,
Its golden hand softly flows,
Bringing life to each tender view.

The shadows play as light cascades,
Across the fields, a gentle dance,
Where every leaf in hue parades,
Awakens dreams in a fleeting glance.

In whispers sweet, the breezes sigh,
While flowers bloom with colors bright,
As heaven's canvas fills the sky,
In strokes of day that banish night.

Yet in this beauty is a breath,
Of transience we come to know,
Each moment dances, lives, then rests,
A fleeting sun in softest glow.

So cherish each, as day does fade,
The veil of light, a tender kiss,
In evening's arms, we're ever swayed,
To find a world of gentle bliss.

Crystalline Frostbite

The morning dawns with icy breath,
A crystalline world, a sharp delight,
Where frost decorates in quiet death,
And bites the skin with chilling might.

Each step in snow, a crunching song,
As whispers echo through the trees,
This beauty sharp, where we belong,
Embraced by nature, sharp as freeze.

The diamonds dance on every bough,
Reflecting sunlight's fleeting grace,
A fleeting kiss upon our brow,
In winter's warm, unyielding embrace.

Yet behind this fragile, frosted veil,
A story woven of wintry strife,
For beauty stings, and yet, we trail,
Through chills and dreams that hold us tight.

So as we wander this frozen land,
With hearts unyielding amidst the frost,
We'll find our way, hand in hand,
Through crystalline worlds, never lost.

Echoes of a Frosty Dawn

In whispers cold, the morning breaks,
A silver veil on frozen lakes.
Soft as breath, the daylight sighs,
As winter's grip in silence lies.

Footprints trace through sparkling snow,
Each step a tale, a dance, a glow.
The world awakes, the shadows flee,
In frosty light, I feel so free.

Trees stand tall in crystal crowns,
Guarding secrets of the towns.
The air, a crisp and vibrant song,
Where all the dreams of winter throng.

Echoes linger, soft yet bright,
Painting scenes in morning light.
A promise held in each new ray,
That spring awaits, not far away.

So let me breathe this frosty air,
With each exhale, I shed my care.
For in this moment, time stands still,
And heart embraces winter's chill.

Glacial Elegy

Beneath the ice, a world concealed,
Where time and space remain unsealed.
A silent hymn of ages past,
In glacial depths, memories last.

Frosted branches arch with grace,
As winter's breath finds its place.
A tranquil scene, a frozen sigh,
In shadowed light, the echoes lie.

Crystal shards like stars above,
Reflecting whispers of lost love.
In every flake, a soul remembers,
The warmth of days in soft Decembers.

Nature pens her quiet rhyme,
Each icy note a dance with time.
With fragile beauty shrouded deep,
In dreams of warmth, the shadows seep.

Yet in this cold, a spark remains,
A flicker bright despite the chains.
For in the heart, the fires strive,
In glacial realms, we learn to thrive.

Frostbitten Fantasies

In the twilight's grip, dreams entwine,
Where frostbitten wishes silently shine.
Whispers of hope in the chilly night,
Dance like fairies in silver light.

Sparkling gems on branches hung,
A fairy tale yet to be sung.
With every breath, enchantments sail,
Carried softly on winter's gale.

Snowflakes twirl like dancer's feet,
In a world where cold and magic meet.
Underneath vast, starry skies,
Lie the secrets no one denies.

Fingers trace the icy panes,
Sketching wishes, joy, and pains.
In each formation, dreams reside,
Frostbitten fantasies cannot hide.

So let your heart embrace the chill,
In frozen realms, your spirit will.
For every frosty breath you take,
Awakens dreams that never break.

The Stillness of December

In December's hush, the world holds tight,
Blanketed by a starry night.
Silence woven through frosty air,
A tender peace beyond compare.

Snowflakes whisper as they descend,
Magical notes the cold winds send.
Each flake a story of where it's been,
In the quiet, soft moments, din.

The glow of lanterns, warm and bright,
Guide us through the chilly night.
In every corner, shadows play,
Telling tales of the fading day.

Stillness wraps around the trees,
As nature sleeps in frosty ease.
In every breath, the chill reminds,
Of beauty in the silence, confined.

So savor now the quiet grace,
In December's tender embrace.
For in this stillness, hearts will learn,
The warmth of love, when seasons turn.

Frosty Reveries

The air is crisp, the world is white,
Crisp leaves crackle, fading light.
Through branches bare, the shadows play,
Whispers of frost lead thoughts astray.

Moonlight glimmers on the frost,
In this stillness, nothing's lost.
Stars above in silence gleam,
Wrapped in winter's gentle dream.

A breath of steam escapes my lips,
Winter's kiss in frosty nips.
I wander through this quiet night,
Embraced by frost, the world feels right.

The crunch of snow beneath my feet,
Echoes softly, bittersweet.
Memories dance like flurries bright,
In the heart of a winter's night.

Nature sleeps with peaceful grace,
In this winter, time finds space.
Frosty dreams, they swirl and weave,
In the magic, I believe.

The Gathering Chill

As daylight dims, the shadows grow,
A breath of winter's chill does flow.
Leaves surrendered to earth's embrace,
Nature dons her silvery lace.

Clouds gather dark, a somber shroud,
The whispers of winter, quiet yet loud.
Jackets drawn close, we huddle tight,
Against the chill of an approaching night.

Fires crackle, warmth sought inside,
While snowflakes dance, a gentle tide.
Each flake unique, a crafted spell,
Filling our hearts with stories to tell.

The world dressed in a frosty gleam,
In the distance, a flickering beam.
As evening sets, the chill does rise,
A stark beauty beneath the skies.

Hearts are warmed by tales old and new,
Gathering strength when skies turn blue.
In this gathering chill, we unite,
Thanks to the frost, we find our light.

Songs of the Frozen Wind

Whispers through the barren trees,
Songs carried by the winter breeze.
A melody sharp, crisp, and rare,
The frozen wind sings everywhere.

Echoes of frost dance on the air,
A haunting tune, both sweet and fair.
With every gust, the notes take flight,
A symphony woven into the night.

With chattering teeth, we listen close,
Nature's concert, we adore the most.
In swirling snow, the music sways,
Guiding our hearts through winter's maze.

Hushed tones of night, the stars attend,
In frozen silence, the songs blend.
Each flurry brings a voice anew,
Carried softly, like morning dew.

The world is still, a heart in trance,
Caught in the wind's mesmerizing dance.
The songs of winter, pure and bright,
Lead us forth into the night.

A Tapestry of Ice

A canvas blank, all white and bare,
The world adorned with frosty flair.
Each blade of grass, a crystal gem,
Nature's art, a shimmering diadem.

Icicles hanging, fragile threads,
Glistening where the sunlight spreads.
A tapestry spun with winter's hand,
Beauty weaves across the land.

The lakes lie still, a glassy sheen,
Reflecting wonders, soft and serene.
Under the moon, the world does shine,
In this icy glow, our hearts entwine.

Snowflakes drift like whispered dreams,
Each a wonder, or so it seems.
Falling gently, a lover's sigh,
Kissing the earth as they pass by.

Embroidered skies, clouds holding fast,
Hues of winter, fading light cast.
In this tapestry of ice we dwell,
Each moment frozen, stories to tell.

Milton Keynes UK
Ingram Content Group UK Ltd.
UKHW010228111224
452348UK00011B/593